LOUIS McGUFFIE VC

THE STORY OF WIGTOWN'S WAR HERO

MIKE MORLEY
& JACK HUNTER

First published 2018 by
Royal Burgh of Wigtown & District Community Council

"To the loved ones who waited at home"

British Library Cataloguing-in-Publication Data

A catalogue record for this book is available from the British Library

ISBN 978-1-5272-1874-1

Book design by Michael Marshall, Breathing Space Productions

Printed at Newton Stewart by JB Print

*Cover Photograph of Louis McGuffie taken from "War History of the 5th Battalion King's Own
Scottish Borderers" by G F Scott Elliot.*

LOUIS McGUFFIE VC

Contents

FOREWORD

It has been estimated that almost 700,000 Scots served in the First World War and around 135,000 died. 74 Scots won the Victoria Cross out of a total of 627 awarded during the conflict. This book is an attempt to provide the background to one of the men whose valour was recognised by the highest military honour. Up to the outbreak of war in August 1914 Louis McGuffie probably lived an unremarkable life in a small town in South West Scotland. Just over four years later he had shown extreme courage and had survived fierce fighting in parts of the world he had probably never even heard of. He died only six weeks before the Armistice that brought the fighting to an end.

I had been bitten by the military research bug three years after retiring and moving to Wigtown. Why I can't quite recall but I remember, one day, walking past the war memorial and stopping and wondering just who these men named on it were; men who we say each November 11 we will remember.

"Someone should find out about them", I thought. I admit it took a few weeks before I realised I should be "Someone". Fortunately I soon found the website of the Scottish Military History Group dedicated to investigating all the military memorials in the country. It provided both vital information and friendly encouragement. My research gradually evolved into examining all those with Wigtown connections who served in the Great War (over 230 men and 2 women - but still counting!). Of course, Louis McGuffie and his family fell within that research.

The Government's announcement of ways to commemorate the First World War included the laying of commemorative paving slabs on the 100th anniversary of the award of the Victoria Cross to each brave individual. I was invited to join a working group to determine the best location of the Louis McGuffie slab and the activities to mark that centenary. Local historian, Jack Hunter, had led a discussion at the 2015 Wigtown Book Festival about the Wigtown of Louis McGuffie's time and kindly offered his notes should we want to produce some sort of commemorative publication. These notes form the bulk of Chapter Two. As I had undertaken the family research I agreed to pull something together and this is what we have ended up with!

I hope that I have conveyed some feel for the times when Louis was growing up - his family circumstances, the town where he worked and played. Information on his war service is patchy but I have attempted to stitch together his journey from home to the Dardanelles, Egypt, Palestine, France and Belgium.

Through it all I have also included reference to some of the other brave men of Wigtown who went off to fight. When news reached Wigtown of both Louis's valour and his death the town rallied around his widowed mother. Townsfolk helped pay for her trip to Buckingham Palace to receive the Victoria Cross in Louis's stead and, a few years later, proudly displayed a memorial plaque to him. The pride felt by the community has, I hope, been re-ignited today.

Louis's bravery also touched individuals within his family. I was privileged to meet a veteran of D-Day who had driven, at the age of 90, from his home in Lanarkshire to Wigtown to find out who the hero in his family was. He had grown up with stories of Louis McGuffie and his Victoria Cross but had never been able to find out how he was related. It turns out that he was a descendent of Louis's father's first wife. He went home grateful for a mystery solved.

I'm sure that there is much in this account that I have missed. Any mistakes and errors are entirely mine.

Mike Morley
October 2017
Wigtown

Acknowledgements

I soon discovered that writing a booklet about a local hero is not easy! However, I am grateful to Wigtown's local boy and historian Jack Hunter for providing the text for the chapter about Wigtown. I hope I have been able to emulate the knowledge and humour of that chapter. I'd also like to thank the Working Group, ably chaired by Nick Walker, charged with deciding the siting of the Louis McGuffie VC paving slab, for offering me the opportunity to write this booklet and for their encouragement throughout.

I'd like to thank my wife, Lynn, for putting up with me tapping away on the laptop, for her encouragement, proof reading, photography and suggestions to make this narrative more relevant to present-day readers.

I'd also like to thank another Wigtown boy, David McNally, who appeared on my doorstep one day with the photograph of the opening of Wigtown War Memorial that I have included in this account. David's enthusiasm for local history was infectious. What's more he had been over to Belgium to see the trench system at Bayernwald where Louis won his VC. He told me that, when he arrived, the museum was closed but when folk heard he was from Wigtown they opened it specially for him. Apparently Louis McGuffie and his exploits are known by all in the area.

Thanks, too, to Andy Middlemiss and Ian Martin of the KOSB Association for their helpful input on the regimental aspects. Also to Mike Marshall who has wrestled my draft into a proper book!

Of course, without funding this book would never have seen the light of day so I'd like to thank particularly two organisations which have so generously supported us financially.

The primary funder of this publication is the Galloway Association of Glasgow, to whom we are profoundly grateful. The Association was formed in 1791 evolving into today's independent charitable trust. The Association supports non-commercial good causes within Galloway, particularly the arts, education, non-commercial groups and individuals. Grants are given to young people who need financial support at the commencement of their tertiary education, and to projects that benefit the community, groups or individuals. To find out more please visit their website at *www.gallowayassoc.org.uk*

The Stranraer and District Local History Trust is almost 200 years younger than the Galloway Association of Glasgow. Its objectives are to research, record and publish information on local history for the benefit of the community. Since its foundation the Trust has sold almost 33,000 books, covering every aspect of life and history of the people and places of Stranraer and surrounding district, and has also recorded the stories of working life and leisure of the inhabitants of this corner of Scotland with the creation of a collection of recorded discs and tapes and written manuscripts which are available for public research. Find out more at: *www.stranraerhistory.org.uk*

More generally I'd like to thank the staff at Wigtown Library for helping with the research and, equally, some of the experts on the Scottish Military History Group (you know who you are!).

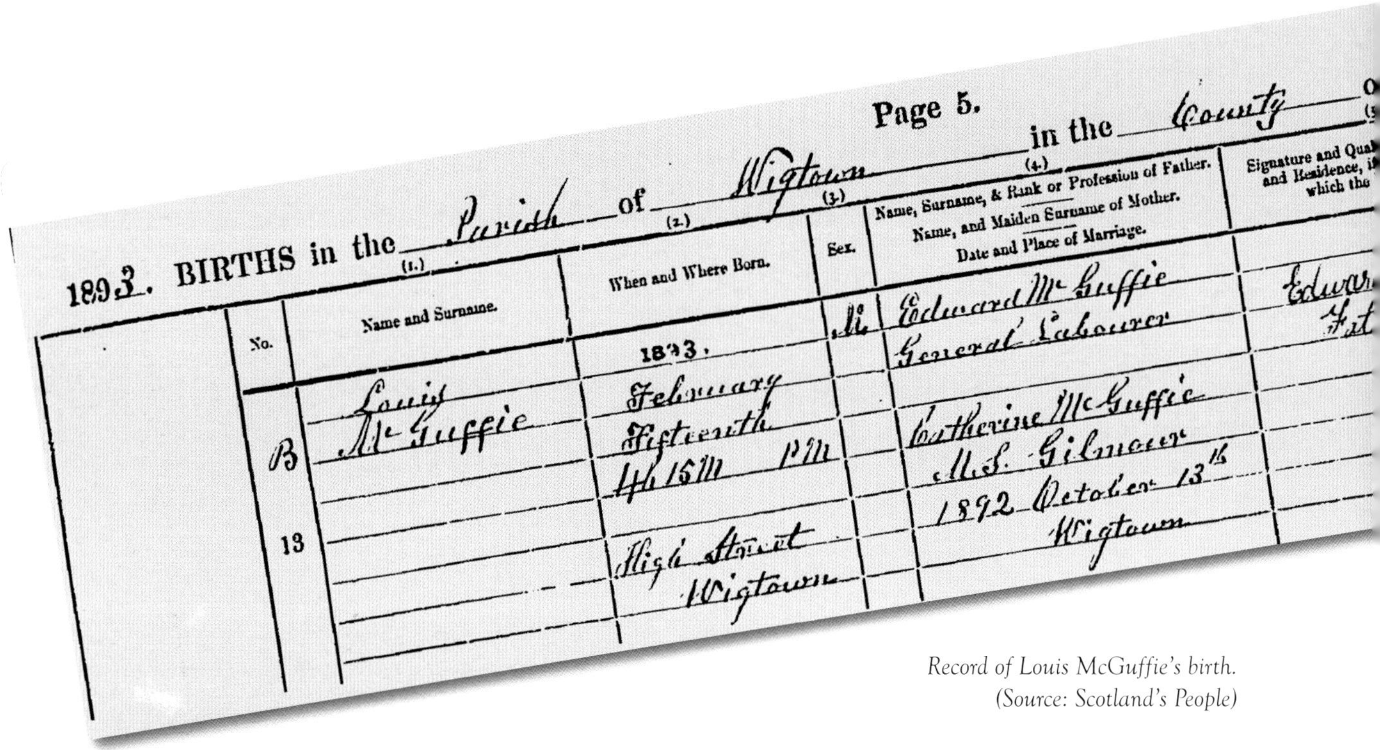

Page 5.

1893. BIRTHS in the Parish (1.) of Wigtown (2.) in the County (3.)

No.	Name and Surname.	When and Where Born.	Sex.	Name, Surname, & Rank or Profession of Father. Name, and Maiden Surname of Mother. Date and Place of Marriage.	Signature and Qual... and Residence, if... which the...
B 13	Louis McGuffie	1893. February Fifteenth 4h 15m PM High Street Wigtown	M	Edward McGuffie General Labourer Catherine McGuffie M.S. Gilmour 1892 October 13th Wigtown	Edwar... Fat...

Record of Louis McGuffie's birth. (Source: Scotland's People)

1 – Louis McGuffie's Family

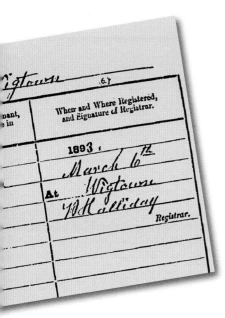

Louis McGuffie was born at 4.15 pm on 15 February 1893 at his grandparents' home on High Street, Wigtown, the son of Edward McGuffie and his wife, Catherine Gilmour.

Although Louis was the first-born child of Edward and Catherine, he "inherited" both half brothers and step-brothers and sisters. (*Appendices 1 to 3 help to explain!*).

Edward had been married before but his first wife, Lilly, had died at the age of 36 in January 1890 from heart disease and ascites of the abdomen, a condition commonly caused by cirrhosis of the liver. Lilly was a Perthshire girl who had come down to Wigtown with her then husband, shepherd Benjamin McCallum. With him she had five children, three boys and two girls, before Benjamin's death around 1880.

Lilly married Edward McGuffie on Christmas Day 1883 and their union produced three boys: Thomas (born 1885), Edward John (born 1886) and James Dornan (born 1889). Tragedy was to strike the family (for the first time), when Lilly's first son, Edward McCallum, died in 1886 at the age of 13: curiously, the local newspaper, in reporting his death, attributed it to eating a large quantity of raw vegetables on the day previous.

By the time of the 1891 census it appears that the McCallum children had found work and left home. David was a general servant to James McRobert in Wigtown High Street; Maggie had obtained similar work at Barrachan, Penninghame; and Elizabeth was a cook and domestic servant in Newton Stewart.

Lilly's death left Edward to look after their three boys aged 5 or less. Doubtless he relied on his parents and extended family to help him with their upbringing but the search for a new wife was probably not far from his mind. His marriage to Catherine Gilmour two years after Lilly's death would be timely and fortunate in that circumstance. The birth of Louis in 1893 was followed by the arrival of twins, Benjamin McCallum McGuffie and Alexander Mitchell McGuffie (in 1895). A further boy, Robert was born in 1898. By then, however, tragedy had struck the family again. At the age of 6 months Benjamin caught bronchitis and, after a 10 day illness, died at the family's home in High Street. The page of the death register recording Benjamin's death contains three deaths within an 11 day period of a 4 day old, an 8 month old (also from bronchitis) and Benjamin. A sobering reminder of child mortality at the end of the nineteenth century.

Record of Benjamin McGuffie's death
(Source: Scotland's People)

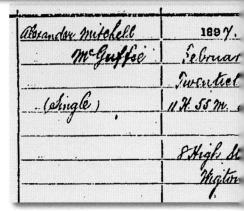

The pain of loss struck again far too quickly. Almost a year to the date that Benjamin died, his twin brother, Alexander, succumbed at the age of 18 months from a kidney illness and congestion of the lungs. Louis would have been 4 years old when Alexander died and the tragedy may have not registered very clearly in his young mind.

Record of Alexander McGuffie's death
(Source: Scotland's People)

| W | 18 months | Edward McGuffie General Labourer | Kidney Disease – several months. Congestion of Lungs – 7 days as certified by R. MacClelland M.D. | | Edward Guffie Father Present | 1897 February 30th At Wigtown James Clark Asst. Registrar |

The McGuffie homes in Wigtown

Census returns show the nomadic life of the McGuffies in Wigtown over Louis's life there as the family migrated from High Street to Low Vennel at the other end of town via Botany Street.

Left: High Street in 1912 looking downhill towards Trammondford

(Source: https://www.facebook.com/treelap/photos)

and below as it is today.

High Street: Although the present day housing stock of High Street has not changed significantly, most of the McGuffie homes there have been demolished. Louis was born at number 21 (gone) and Benjamin died at number 25 (also gone). In 1897, the year of Alexander's death, the family were living at number 8 which can still be seen. The photograph above of the 1912 Root Show and Parade is taken in High Street with the junction with Botany Street just slightly behind and to the right of the horse. The houses up the steps on the right with the group of girls looking on are probably numbers 23 and 25.

Right: Botany Street looking downhill towards High Vennel around the start of the 20ᵗʰ Century
(*Source: Old Wigtown*)

and below as it is today.

Botany Street: By 1898 and the birth of Robert, the McGuffies had moved to Botany Street, where the town's most impoverished citizens lived. The photograph above looks down the Street. The building in the right foreground is the Poor House which, at the 1901 census, is recorded as 22 Botany Street. Robert McGuffie was born at number 18 which may be just a couple of doors down. Few of the buildings of the time remain today.

Low Vennel: By the time of the 1901 census the McGuffies had moved to 20 Low Vennel. Ten years later they were living at number 21. Edward McGuffie's death in 1917 is recorded as at number 19. The photograph opposite was taken between 1905 and 1914. So we may be looking at the McGuffie boys standing in the street. Most of the housing in Low Vennel has been demolished. Numbers 14 and 16 still exist, giving an indication that the McGuffies lived close to where Barclay's garage (formerly the bus depot) now stands.

Above: Low Vennel circa 1905
(Source: Glimpses of old Wigtownshire)

Left: as it is in the present day.

North Main Street: By 1918 Catherine had moved to number 1 North Main Street. It was here she received the news of Louis's VC award and death. She continued to live here until her death in 1937.

Louis McGuffie's forebears

Census and birth records extending back to the start of the 19th Century show a solid Wigtown and Bladnoch pedigree for the McGuffies.

Edward (Louis's father) was born in 1858 at Bladnoch. He spent most of his life in Wigtown and Bladnoch, with a short adventure to Sorbie, appearing in the 1881 census as a general labourer (his job throughout his life). Edward was the eldest of seven children of Thomas McGuffie and his wife Margaret Ranken who had married in Wigtown in 1857. Thomas (born 1835), too, was firmly rooted in Wigtown, living variously in Bank Street, Bladnoch and High Vennel. He worked as a rural postman. He, in turn, was the eldest son of Edward McGuffie, an agricultural labourer born in 1812, and his wife, Agnes McCaa, who were living in Bladnoch in the 1841 census.

Louis's mother, Catherine Gilmour, was also a Wigtown lass but with a bit more adventure in her own background prior to her marriage to Edward. She was born in 1861 at High Street, Wigtown, the fourth child of Irishman John Gilmour and his wife, Agnes McCallister. In 1871 the Gilmours had moved around the corner to Botany Street. However, when she was in her late teens Catherine went to Liverpool to seek work. The 1881 census shows her working as a domestic servant to the Dockray family at 3 Cornwallis Street, Liverpool. Ten years later she was still away from Wigtown, living at Berkswell, Lanarkshire, where she worked as a cook and domestic servant for a Mr David Bryce and family. In a nod to modern-day Wigtown and its status as Scotland's Book Town, Mr Bryce was a publisher, bookseller and stationer based in Glasgow.

Louis's early years

School - although we have no record of Louis's schooling it is safe to assume he went to Wigtown Burgh School (now Wigtown Primary). We know from the school records that Edward and Catherine were called to the school to explain the erratic attendance of Louis's younger brother, Robert. Robert's absences can probably be explained by him having to work to help supplement the family income. There is no reason to think that the home demands on Louis would be any different. Indeed, the regularity of attendance at school (or lack of it) was something the School Board had been warned about in 1908.

The photograph above is from about 1909, just after Louis would have left, and shows pupils doing drill at the school, which would, doubtless, have helped in Louis's army service.

What happened to Louis's immediate family?

Edward McGuffie died on 20 October 1917 at the age of 59 from a cerebral haemorrhage. The record of his death (below) has an interesting annotation in the first column. Upon investigation it appears that his sudden death must have required an autopsy as the annotation refers to a Precognition report signed off by the Procurator Fiscal.

Catherine died 20 years later in May 1937. Her death was reported in the Galloway Gazette (29/5/1937):

> The death took place on Sunday of Mrs C McGuffie, 1 North Main Street, Wigtown, mother of the late Sergeant Louis McGuffie, 1/5th Battalion, KOSB, who was awarded the Victoria Cross in the Great War for most conspicuous bravery and resourceful leadership near Wytschaete, Belgium, on 28th September 1918, but unfortunately was killed in action on 4th October 1918 unaware of the great honour that he had brought to his native town and also to the local regiment. The late Mrs McGuffie travelled to London to receive this most coveted award at Buckingham Palace from the late King George, in 1919. In the entrance leading to the Town Hall, Wigtown, a bronze-and-marble tablet was erected by the late Sir Peter H McClelland in memory of this heroic soldier. Mrs McGuffie's funeral took place on Wednesday at Wigtown Cemetery and was attended by a large concourse of mourners. The service was conducted by the Rev Gavin Lawson.

Sadly her grave in Wigtown's High Cemetery is not marked.

Thomas McGuffie, Edward's eldest child and half-brother to Louis, had, like Louis, played football for Wigtown Utd before the War. He served with the Army Service Corps, attaining the rank of Sergeant. He married Jane Pretsell and lived in Wigtown's Fountainblue Terrace. He died on 16 March 1959 aged 66 and is buried in Wigtown's High Cemetery.

Edward John, the second child of Edward and Lilly, died in 1955.

James Dornan, Edward and Lilly's third child, died in 1977 at Edinburgh.

Robert, Louis's younger brother, served with the Royal Scots Fusiliers during the war. He was wounded six times and lost an arm in 1917. He became a well-known figure in Wigtown. His love of wild-fowling was not hampered by his disability, Robert compensating for the loss of the limb by the use of a punt gun. Intriguingly, he was on good terms with film actor James Robertson Justice, who owned Orchardton House, just off Agnew Crescent, after the Second World War: the two went shooting game when the actor was in town. Robert married Margaret McGhie. He died on 6 January 1977 aged 79 and is buried in Wigtown High Cemetery.

Robert had inherited Louis's Victoria Cross when his mother died and presented it to the King's Own Scottish Borderers Museum where it can still be seen.

2 - Louis McGuffie's Wigtown

If we could bring Louis McGuffie to stand where his Victoria Cross commemorative slab has been laid, would he recognise the town that he left a hundred years ago? He most probably would, though an exploration beyond the town centre would reveal some changes. The County Buildings have not changed greatly, although the bustle of a county town has quietened. Some familiar buildings such as the Old Red Lion Inn (to his right) and the old dairy and guest house where the Catholic priest lodged (to his left) have been replaced by flats on North and South Main Streets respectively. There are fewer shops and the last of the banks has gone but architecturally the town is largely unchanged. An attempt to visit his former homes in Low Vennel, High Street and Botany Street would find them, for the most part, gone. The school is larger but still on the same site.

The Wigtown of Louis McGuffie had a higher population than the town has today (c1300 against c1100) but was much smaller in extent. The ring of former local authority housing which now partly encircles the town (New Road, Jubilee Terrace, Fountainblue, Lightlands Ave and Terrace, Seaview, Beddie Crescent) had its beginning only in the 1930s: up till then the council housing stock comprised seven properties. Clearly most houses had more occupants than today with many informally divided between two or more families, each with a floor or even part of one shared. For example, the six adults of the McGuffie family occupied a succession of small cottages in Low Vennel. In many cases the houses facing the street are supplemented with further accommodation in the pends to their rear.

In Louis McGuffie's day Wigtown had just passed the peak of its importance and prosperity but was still the major town in Wigtownshire. It retained its traditional role as county town with the Sheriffdom based at the County Buildings but the administrative centre had moved to Stranraer with the creation of the county council in 1890.

For much of the period under review the county clerk was Charles McLean, who also had a legal practice and was manager of the National Bank of Scotland, the latter housed in what is now The Old Bank Bookshop. McLean ran the affairs of Wigtownshire from the small office beside that bookshop together with two modest single-storey houses beyond. Old Wigtown resident Mr Gordon Gardiner remembered going to one of those latter to obtain his motor cycle licence.

Mr McLean's unpretentious empire was completed by a room, now the Cyber centre, in the County Buildings across the road. In the centre can still be seen the walk-in safe which, on one occasion, was the cause of a crisis, when its key was thrown into the harbour by a disaffected and inebriated minor civil servant.

The County Clerk's foothold in the County Buildings was in fact a toehold. Despite its name the primary purpose of the sandstone monolith at the east end of the Square was to house the county's sheriff court. Only two rooms fell outside that role: the already mentioned one and the assembly hall upstairs. Today's assembly hall is a combination of a former courtroom and the sheriff's retiring room. Thus for three hundred years the Agnew family, as hereditary sheriffs of Wigtownshire to 1746, had to make the 60-mile round trip from their Lochnaw home near Leswalt to dispense the sovereign's justice at Wigtown in the present building's previous incarnation. Their possible status as Wigtownshire's first commuters would be a dubious consolation.

As logic therefore dictated, the headquarters of the county constabulary for many years was at Wigtown. The first police HQ was at the top of Bank Street, beside the County Buildings in what is now a block of two private houses. From here it migrated in 1881 to Harbour Road and what had been the prison, still eye-catching for its forest of elongated chimneys. Despite the increased space available there one chief constable pointed out that he did not possess an office of his own. However in 1922 the county police headquarters was moved to Stranraer, a fate shared eventually by Wigtown's other administrative functions.

The Wigtown Louis McGuffie knew was still the service centre for the Machars although its role as a communication hub was fast diminishing with the decline of waterborne transport. Numerous businesses catered for those various functions: three banks, the British Linen, the Clydesdale, and the National Bank of Scotland, complemented by and closely linked with five firms of solicitors, all under the watchful eye of an Inland Revenue office with a staff of three. Catering for more material needs were eleven grocers, nine shoemakers, six carters, five cattle dealers (the survivors of the once thriving cattle trade) and, intriguingly, one bird stuffer.

The presence of four ministers and three precentors in an 1877 directory testifies to a strong, if diversified, religious life. The parish church still stands where Louis McGuffie would have known it and he may have known the minister for the Rev Gavin Lawson also served as a combatant in the Great War, preaching in his sergeant's uniform when on leave. However the site of the Free Church in Harbour Road, almost opposite South Back Street, is now occupied by a private house, though its Roll of Honour, listing men from the congregation who served in the war, can still be seen in the parish church.

The Free Church's own Minister, James Fordyce, who had arrived in the town from Australia in 1911, would see service in the Argyll and Sutherland Highlanders during the war. No trace remains of the United Presbyterian building in Fountainblue, beside Craigmount Guest House. The Roman Catholic chapel in South Main Street was still fairly new in Louis McGuffie's day, having been built in 1879, and a congregation of Plymouth Brethren existed until 1916. While the number of denominations represented in the town is the same today as then, the earlier congregations were much larger: the parish and U.P. churches both had seating for 600 while the Free Church required the services of an assistant minister.

Louis McGuffie would attend Wigtown public school, the oldest in the county. The present building dates from 1846 but is now much expanded. In 1898, the year Louis would have started school, a new headmaster, Mr James Edward, was appointed. It was a year of change at the school: an Education Department report had criticised the very limited range of instruction for Secondary Subjects, leading to the resignation of Mr Edward's predecessor and a number of other teachers. The young McGuffie would leave school at thirteen, the statutory leaving age, having received his entire education at Wigtown.

At the time he left school a former soldier, Sgt MacFarlane, was appointed for the instruction of "Physical Exercise and Military Drill" (as well as being janitor and school attendance officer). He may also have noticed the rather dilapidated state the building had fallen into. In 1909 the School Board appointed a committee to supervise the cleaning and repair of the school during the summer vacation. The committee drew attention to a very large number of broken panes of glass requiring attention and recommended that the Headmaster should investigate these "accidents" and punish the offenders. The committee also reported the condition of the playground due to horses and cattle being grazed there after school hours.

Either because he was not selected or, equally probably, did not wish to go, Louis did not attend the Ewart High School in Newton Stewart. When war broke out at least three Wigtown school staff joined the Army: Mr MacFarlane, the janitor; Mr Sutherland, principal teacher of English; and Mr McGeoch who would go on to be awarded the Distinguished Conduct Medal during the conflict.

Job prospects in the Wigtown of Louis's day were reasonable. We know from the 1911 census that he became a general labourer like his father and brothers. However, other possibilities existed. Agriculture was a major employer in the Machars while a variety of small industries were located in Wigtown's industrial suburb, Bladnoch. The Scottish Co-operative Wholesale Society creamery there, founded in 1899, had a workforce of 90. Louis McGuffie's uncle Thomas worked there and the creamery would provide almost 30 of its workforce for the Army. (A 1927 film, available on-line from the National Library of Scotland, provides a snapshot of the Creamery in full operation as well as the countryside around Bladnoch. It is unlikely that much will have changed in the dozen or so years since Louis McGuffie's time) The nearby distillery, then owned by the founding McClelland family, offered an admittedly somewhat precarious 20 jobs. The village was also home to a foundry and a coachworks, while just outside it another McClelland family enterprise, a potato mill, produced not only potato flour but, more exotically, champagne and wine. To cater for all alcoholic preferences, Wigtown itself boasted a small brewery in Botany Street.

Also to be found in Botany Street was the town's poorhouse which catered for the impoverished and needy. The 1901 census identifies two youngsters living there who would later serve in Louis McGuffie's regiment, the King's Own Scottish Borderers. One-year old James Hargreaves lived there with his mother, Jane, who was the keeper of the poorhouse.

He served with the 1st Battalion and was killed in action in August 1918 aged 18. James Douglas Gilmour was also living at the poorhouse at the time of the 1901 census with his parents and three siblings. He served throughout the war, becoming the "batman" of General Egerton before being invalided out of the army in August 1918.

In that pre-National Health Service age social welfare was provided by private individuals and agencies and Louis McGuffie's Wigtown seems to have been fairly well supplied. Dr McBride was followed by Dr Lilico who arrived in Wigtown shortly before the Great War and who practised until after the Second World War, with a two-year break for his service in the Royal Army Medical Corps when the town was left with no medical cover at all. Both doctors practised from 11 North Main Street before Dr Lilico built "Benvoir" (complete with surgery) at the corner of Lightlands Terrace and Lightlands Avenue. William Lilico is commemorated in a street name (Lilico Loaning), and bred Border Terriers which had a strong antipathy to silence. From 1908, when Louis was fifteen, additional medical provision was available from the Wigtown and District Nursing Association. A further alternative could be found in the local newspapers which were full of advertisements for various quack remedies and dental supplies such as a full set of teeth for £2 2s (£2.10p) offering a "choice assortment of teeth".

A Clothing Club and a Coal Club were intended to combat poverty while the spiritual wellbeing of the community was the concern of the Good Templar Lodge and its junior section, each with 100 members. Those who remember Louis's youngest brother, Robert, may speculate whether the last two organisations featured "Duckins" on the membership rolls.

The Friendly Society, established in 1795 and possessing 51 members in 1850, may still have been in existence 43 years later when Louis was born; a branch, founded in 1873, of the Independent Order of Oddfellows continued its benevolent work during his lifetime, holding its annual Root Show and Sports Day on Southfield Park. The Chain of Office of the Oddfellows can still be seen in the museum inside the County Buildings.

Wigtown Utd, 1913-14 Galloway Shield Winners
(Source: Wigtown & Bladnoch FC)

Turn-of-the-century Wigtown appears to have developed an active social, leisure, and community life. Louis McGuffie played for one of Wigtown's football teams, either the summer league outfit, the trophy-winning junior side, or the senior team, which competed in the Southern Counties League and had its ground, as is the case today, at Trammondford Park.

The photograph opposite from early 1914 shows the team, which does not include Louis McGuffie, in front of the County Buildings holding the recently won Galloway Shield. All the players and the trainer (but not the chap posed with his hat at a jaunty angle!) were to serve in the war but not all would return. The grandstand at the team's Trammondford ground was traditionally the unauthorised venue for Sunday games of pitch-and-toss. More respectable sporting activities included bowling and tennis, which shared the central square, quoiting at Bladnoch Bridge, and billiards. A brass band and pipe band regularly displayed their skills at the bandstand in the town centre probably disturbing the peace in the nearby public library, which had existed since 1794. The bass drum and a bugle from the band can still be seen in the museum in the County Buildings.

Indoor activities also flourished. The occasional poems of unofficial town laureate Gordon Fraser reveal a calendar of concerts, presentation dinners, annual functions of various organisations, and regular meetings of the Debating Club, and the Young Men's Mutual Improvement Association. (Hindsight assures us that the latter body could have had nothing to teach Louis McGuffie!) The premises of the local Masonic Lodge are still to be seen in Agnew Crescent.

Like generations of local youngsters the young McGuffies would have found a tempting variety of activities in the vicinity of the nearby village of Bladnoch. A red letter day was the occasional arrival of the barley boat with its load for Bladnoch distillery. Its attraction was not its modest size but that it came up the river almost to the village, berthing at a small stone quay just before the creamery, attended from the harbour by a crowd of excited young Wigtonians.

The stretch of water just below the road bridge was by tradition taken over in the Easter holidays by a horde of would-be anglers armed with improvised tackle. It is doubtful if their endeavours had any noticeable effect on stocks of the famous Bladnoch salmon or greatly concerned the Earl of Galloway, owner of the fishing rights.

A few hundred yards upstream of the bridge a small bay of mud and shingle, called Linghour, provided the main bathing facilities in the neighbourhood: even now many Wigtonians remember learning to swim there. Access from the village was by a narrow path between the river and distillery lade, going "up the Cut" being a local synonym for going swimming. It is one of life's ironies that the superlative achievements of Louis McGuffie have inspired no local poet while the imperfect attractions of Linghour have.

Another, more hazardous location for a dip was Wigtown harbour. A June 1910 edition of the Wigtownshire Free Press carried a report of the rescue from drowning in the Harbour of a young man called A J Hannah. He and three friends had been bathing there when he got into difficulties; fortunately one of his companions, Norman Todd, was a strong swimmer and saved his life: Norman was to receive an award by the Royal Humane Society and a Carnegie Award for bravery. He and his four brothers would all see active service in the War.

While water for recreational purposes abounded in Bladnoch, neighbouring Wigtown was less happily endowed with water for domestic and community use. No gravitation water supply existed until 1931, when a pipeline was built to bring water fourteen miles from a burn on the upper slopes of Cairnsmore of Fleet across the bay.

Until then springs and wells continued to perform the role they had for hundreds of years. Among the most used were the pumps on either side of the Square opposite New Road and the one at Ballgreen close to the old harbour.

The well at Ballgreen today.

In addition to public supplies several buildings had their own private source. "Fairholme", next to the County Buildings, had a pump in the garden just outside the back door while the former parish church manse on Church Lane had an en-suite well in the kitchen. Like others of his generation Louis McGuffie would have had to take his turn fetching pails of water from the street pump.

Wigtown's ratepayers took part in their own referendum in 1912 over their water supply. They were given the option of either the gravitational supply (which eventually arrived almost twenty years later) or the development of further wells. The local press expressed some scepticism about the latter option pointing out that the Council had spent £61 in 1898 boring for water on Windy Hill. A 52ft deep bore hole only managed to supply water at one gallon every five minutes. As far back as 1884 a report on the wells at Botany Street, High Vennel, Harbour Road and Bank Street recommended discontinuation of the use of the water for dietetic purposes. "Harbour Road," it stated, "contained certain things which showed it was not desirable water for household use. Bank Street was much more impure and beyond all question unfit for domestic use." In 1893 the water at North Back Street (which could have been the McGuffies' nearest water source when they lived at Low Vennel) was reported to be very highly contaminated with organic impurities, apparently of animal origin. The water supply was to be the subject of regular Council debate right up to the start of the war.

In 1931 the county began to receive an electricity supply provided by the Wigtownshire Electricity Company, part of the GEC empire. However since 1925 Wigtown parish church had been lit by electricity courtesy of its own generator.

The use of electricity received a major boost in 1935 when the Galloway Water Power Company commissioned the first of its chain of generating stations in the Ken-Dee valley. A gas supply had been available since 1846, when the Wigtown Gas Company was formed. Originally a private concern, it was taken over by the town council in the 1920s.

Thanks to its efforts Louis McGuffie would never know anything but well lit streets and the lamplighter with his pole would be a familiar figure. The gasworks at the head of Low Vennel was a familiar and conveniently situated sight (and probably smell) to the future hero. Also familiar would have been the horse-drawn burgh dust cart, both based in the burgh yard at the corner of New Road and Lochancroft Lane, on ground now occupied by flats.

The one organisation to which we know with certainty Louis McGuffie belonged was the local Territorial Volunteers. Until 1908, before he enrolled, these part-time soldiers joined the Wigtown section of the Newton Stewart Company of Galloway Rifle Volunteers with its headquarters at the Victoria Hall, now part of the Victoria Arms, opposite the Cree Bridge. Here the volunteers engaged in both military and social pursuits. However the Wigtown section also used the County Buildings in their own town as drill hall and armoury. They practised their sharpshooting on ranges at Kirwaugh and Maidland. They also played their part in the national celebrations such as Queen Victoria's Diamond Jubilee and Edward VII's coronation, with a contingent of local men assisting in the lining of the streets. In 1908 the Galloway Rifle Volunteers were disbanded and replaced by H Company, 5th Battalion (T.F.), The King's Own Scottish Borderers. Its muster roll carries the name of the future V.C.

Many locals took advantage of the relatively cheap passages offered by the steam ship companies to the United States and British Empire to seek their fortunes abroad. For example, a 1908 edition of the local newspaper offered third class travel to Quebec for £5 10s (£5.50p) with the Donaldson Line. A monthly service was offered to New Zealand, Tasmania and Cape Town with booking through a local agent in Newton Stewart. The Allan Line offered sailings to Boston, Philadelphia, New York and half a dozen other North American destinations.

Wigtown Gasworks. (Source: Old Wigtown)

Many of Louis McGuffie's contemporaries found the draw of the New World too tempting to resist though many returned to serve their mother country when war broke out.

John Murray Gow, who had lived in Harbour Road before emigrating to New Zealand, returned as a Private in the Canterbury Regiment only to die in July 1915 in the Gallipoli campaign. Arthur Todd, one of five Todd brothers who had grown up at Dunure on Station Road and served their country, returned with the Australian Forces, was decorated for bravery and survived the war, returning to his new home. Thomas McCheyne, John McDowall, Alexander Laurie and Alexander Broadfoot had all emigrated to Canada only to perish in the conflict: all had Wigtown connections.

Louis McGuffie and his contemporaries were probably unaware they were living in a town whose halcyon days were over and a long, slow decline beginning. The cause was the transformation of the national communications system brought about by two new forms of motive power, the steam engine and the internal combustion engine. The long era of primacy of water-based communications gave way to that of railways and roads. Despite an inadequate harbour Wigtown was well integrated into the former network but on the remote periphery of the latter.

When the railway eventually came to the town amid premature rejoicing in 1875 it was merely a branch line of the main line from Dumfries through Newton Stewart to Stranraer and Ireland, which had been opened fourteen years before. Isolated and out on a limb, Wigtown gradually lost its functions to Newton Stewart and Stranraer and lapsed into obscurity until 1998 and its metamorphosis into Scotland's national book town.

Cap Badge of The King's Own Scottish Borderers

3 · Louis McGuffie's War Service

Louis McGuffie's wartime service was with the King's Own Scottish Borderers. The Regiment can trace its lineage back to 1689 with the Earl of Leven's Regiment of Foot. However, Louis's Battalion, the 1/5th, has its origins with the Galloway Rifle Volunteer Corps of 1881. The Rifles were arranged into 7 companies stretching from Stranraer in the West to Maxwelltown in the East. The Newton Stewart Company included sections from Wigtown, Whithorn, and Creetown.

Boer War

Louis would have been 6 years old when Britain and the Boers went to war in October 1899. The British were embarrassed in the first few weeks of the conflict with the towns of Mafeking, Kimberley and Ladysmith laid siege to. To bolster the numbers of soldiers being sent to South Africa the Volunteer Battalions were called upon to seek men willing to join the Regiments of the Line. Over the course of the three years of the conflict three companies of men from the Galloway Rifle Volunteers sailed for South Africa. They acquitted themselves with distinction. Three Wigtown men, John McMillan, Thomas Rankine and Colin Christison are known to have been part of the Galloway contingent. Even though he would be unaware of much of what was going on, Louis is likely to have picked up the excitement and tension in Wigtown as news came in.

Formation of the Territorial Force

It was the Boer War, and the lessons learned from it, that led to a series of major reforms to the British Army. These changes brought the formation of a permanent expeditionary force prepared and ready to intervene abroad in a major war (as it did in August 1914).

To ensure that home security was maintained if that expeditionary force was called into action, a new Territorial Force was formed from the Volunteer Force and the Yeomanry. As a consequence, in 1908 the Galloway Rifle Volunteer Force became the territorial force for the King's Own Scottish Borderers (apart from the Stranraer Company which supported the Royal Scots Fusiliers). At the time of the reforms the KOSB had two regular battalions (the 1st and 2nd) and a reserve battalion (the 3rd Special Reserve). On 1 April 1908 the newly reformed volunteers became the Regiment's 4th and 5th Battalions.

Service with Wigtown's Volunteers and Territorials required regular drill in the County Buildings, with an annual inspection of the Company's proficiency.

Photograph courtesy of Albanich: History of the Galloway Rifle Volunteers

There was also compulsory attendance at training camp. Weapons training was, of course, also integral and there would have been much use of the ranges at Maidland and Kirwaugh.

Contemporary maps show the rifle range between the railway line and the shore about 200 yards south of the Martyrs' Stake. Firing appears to have been aimed at a flag pole set in the marsh directly in line with Creetown!

To ensure that rifle skills were well honed a variety of competitions were held at all levels from Company against Company at a local level right up to national inter-Regimental matches.

The photograph opposite from 1907 shows the Wigtown section of the Volunteers, proud winners of the Parker-Jarvis Cup, a marksmanship competition between local Companies. (Back row, far left, is Corporal (later Sergeant) William Edwards who would serve alongside Louis McGuffie in the 1/5th KOSB until he was killed at Gallipoli.)

Life in the Territorial Volunteers would have afforded the opportunity to travel across the whole of Britain to camps and competitions whether shooting, cycling or football.

5th Battalion King's Own Scottish Borderers

The Wigtown detachment of the 5th KOSB joined with detachments from Newton Stewart, Whithorn, Creetown, Kirkcowan and Garlieston to become "H" Company, headquartered at Newton Stewart. So it was "H" Company that Louis McGuffie joined, trained and exercised with other young men from the Machars.

At the outbreak of war the existing, first-line Territorial units (including "H" Company) were immediately mobilised. A second line of Territorials was raised in August and September. Louis enlisted a little later on 28 October. As a consequence the first-line Battalions were re-numbered with the 5th KOSB becoming the 1/5th (the Battalion Louis served in), while the second-line Battalion became the 2/5th.

Territorials outside County Buildings, Wigtown.
Source: https://www.facebook.com/treelap/photos

It was with much excitement and optimism that Wigtown, like the rest of the country, mobilised. A report from the Wigtownshire Free Press of 13 August 1914 gives a feel for the mood as the men left town for training at Stirling on Thursday 6 August.

WIGTOWN.

Enthusiastic scenes were witnessed at the County Buildings on Thursday afternoon, the occasion being the departure of 12 local Territorials to join the company at Newton-Stewart. When it became known that the Whithorn and Garlieston sections were to join the Wigtown detachment at two o'clock and proceed to headquarters, Provost Shaw kindly gave an order to Mr R. Jones, Commercial Hotel, to entertain 50 men to dinner. Much to the disappointment of the inhabitants of the Royal Burgh the arrangements were cancelled at the last moment, and the outlying sections were conveyed by motor direct to Newton-Stewart. The local "Terriers" along with the Provost, Magistrates and Councillors, etc., sat down to an excellent luncheon purveyed by Mr Jones. The Provost occupied the chair and proposed the toasts of the "King" and "Territorials," which were enthusiastically received. Sergt. Edwards suitably replied. Before leaving the whole company sang the National Anthem. The section was then photographed in front of the County Buildings, after which they marched round the Square headed by the Burgh Brass Band and followed by a very large crowd. Amid much hand shaking, good wishes, and cheering the men left by motor cars, the departure of which was the signal for an outburst of enthusiasm. Three motor drivers were also entertained and left with 4 o'clock train.

The 1/5th at Newton Stewart
(Source: https://www.facebook.com/treelap/photos)

On arrival at Newton Stewart the Wigtown section joined the rest of their "H" Company comrades ready for onward movement but not before they assembled at the end of Cree Bridge for a photograph. With such a number of men, and the photograph not captioned, it is not possible to be absolutely sure where Louis is in the group. My own opinion, from close inspection, is that he is in the back row (as indicated), bareheaded and probably seeing his colleagues off to training camp. Perhaps their celebrations in the burgh had delayed the Wigtown section requiring them to fall in at the back: for certain Sergeant Edwards, who, as reported above, had responded to the toasts, is towards the back - his moustache is very distinctive!

The 1/5th in the Great War

Following assembly at Newton Stewart the Company travelled by train to Dumfries where the Battalion prepared for training. On 18 August they moved to Bannockburn but found the billets there unfit for troops so they marched the 12 miles to Tillicoultry where their training began. On 3 November they moved on to North Queensferry by train, remaining there until April 1915, then a further transfer to Stirling for a month before moving by train to Liverpool on 19 May. Apparently Liverpool was chaotic with soldiers being assembled for the transfer to the Mediterranean.

On 20 May, Louis and his Battalion embarked on the *Mauretania* and arrived at the island of Lemnos on 28 May. After a short stay there, the 1/5th King's Own Scottish Borderers, part of the 155th Infantry Brigade, landed at Sedd-el-Behr on the Gallipoli Peninsula on 6 June 1915. Here they were engaged in trench warfare against the Turks until early 1916 when they sailed to Port Said where they took up the defence of the Suez Canal and a railway line being laid from Egypt to Palestine.

They took part in the Battle of Romani and the advance across the desert to Palestine, engaging in the 2nd and 3rd Battles of Gaza before seizing key positions in Jerusalem. After the German offensive in Spring 1918 they sailed from Egypt and landed in France on 11 April, joining the line at Vimy. They took part in the advance over the Ypres-Comines Canal and the final drive through Belgium.

Gallipoli

The campaign to capture the Turkish-held Dardanelles was supported by First Sea Lord, Winston Churchill, as a means to support Russia and to force the Turks out of the war. The aim was for Royal Navy ships to force their way through the Straits of Dardanelles and capture the Turkish capital, Constantinople. It failed. So an amphibious landing was planned beginning in late April. Although a toehold on the Gallipoli Peninsula was secured the Allied troops were pinned down on the beaches. The 1/5th KOSB were part of the reinforcing group that sailed from Liverpool on 20 May aboard the *Mauretania*, arriving at Lemnos on 28 May and landing at Gallipoli on 6 June.

Gallipoli 1915 (Source: Online Gallery, www.kosb.co.uk)

A series of assaults against the Turks resulted in little except high casualties. These losses were compounded by heat, flies and lack of sanitation. A shortage of supplies and drinking water was ever-present. The grand assault on the Peninsula rapidly degenerated to trench warfare with the opposing trenches being much closer together than those in France. Rather gruesomely sandbags protecting the trenches were supplemented with dead bodies. Louis and his 1/5th comrades first saw action in the Battle of Gully Ravine as June turned into July. Two of his Wigtown companions, brothers Edward and William Kilpatrick, were both wounded, with the former dying on 4 July.

Two more Wigtown men died just over a week later in the action at Achi Baba Nullah: Sergeant William Edwards was killed on 12 July, leaving a wife and three children; 22 year old James McNeil died two days later. Edwards and McNeil had worked together at Bladnoch Creamery.

A contemporary account from the Battalion provides us with a snapshot of the trials that the soldiers faced; the author is not known nor the town to which he is referring but it could apply to Wigtown as much as any other:

> *News is gradually filtering through regarding the work of the King's Own Scottish Borderers at the Dardanelles. It is a grand record, a story of continual hardship, a prolonged test of nerve and stamina, which the lads of this town and the immediate district are passing with honours. Only a short time ago the cynic delighted to call them "Fireside soldiers" but in the light of recent events the cynic might well hide his diminished head. Our Territorials only awaited their opportunity. It came with overwhelming suddenness, but it found them none-the-less ready, and since our townsmen marched away that day of August to fit themselves for the struggle that was before them, and since they set foot on foreign soil on the 29th of May, they have made for themselves a path of glory. For many it has led to the grave.*

Sickness claimed many lives. October saw a change in the weather with hot days and freezing cold nights, exacerbated by swarms of flies and mosquitoes, dirt and contaminated water, all affecting the general health of the troops. For example, on 13 November the Battalion had 223 men fit to fight but another 212 sick in hospital. Another former Creamery worker, Thomas McCaskie, was evacuated from the Dardanelles suffering from dysentery and brought back to hospital in Southampton for treatment. He failed to recover and died in November. He is buried in Wigtown's High Cemetery.

The local newspaper reported:

> *The funeral took place on Thursday, and was very largely attended, among those present being several of Corporal McCaskie's comrades who are at present invalided home from the Dardanelles. The remains were accompanied to Wigtown Cemetery by the Town Band playing the Dead March from "Saul". The utmost sympathy is felt for the bereaved parents and family. As a mark of respect all places of business were closed during the funeral service.*

It was towards the end of the Gallipoli campaign, shortly prior to evacuation, that the bravery of Louis McGuffie was first reported. An extract from the historical archive of the KOSB describes the events of 29 December:

> *When the mine under G11a exploded the party rushed through the opening and into the enemy trench, taking possession. We were now put to dig a new communication trench, and on the counter-attack by the Turks we manned the parapets and assisted in repelling the attack. Near us our bombing detachment, also attached to the Fusiliers, did magnificent service. Lance-Corpl McMurray was shot through the head by a sniper whilst throwing a continuous series of bombs during a strong Turkish counter-attack. He was ably seconded by Pte McGuffie, who later won the VC in France.*
>
> (Taken from "Answering The Call: Auchencairn and the First World War" by Stuart Wilson.)

Louis did not go through the Gallipoli campaign unscathed. Indeed, he may well have been wounded in his brave action of 29 December as the *Dumfries and Galloway Standard* (Wednesday 26 January 1916) reported:

> **PRIVATE L. McGUFFIE, WIGTOWN.**
> Mr and Mrs McGuffie, Low Vennel, Wigtown, have received official intimation that their son, Private L. McGuffie, 1/5th KOSB, has been wounded at the Dardanelles. This is the second time he has been wounded.

Conditions continued to worsen with heavy rain and snow inundating trenches while strong winds made landing essential supplies more difficult. This, and the lack of military progress, led to the abandonment of the campaign. On 6 January 1916 Louis and the 1/5th were evacuated from the peninsula aboard the *SS Partridge* and moved for duty in Egypt. Five of his Wigtown companions had been killed and a number of others seriously wounded and sick. In total, of 50 officers and 1082 men, the 1/5th had lost 30 officers and 760 men killed, wounded and sick during the campaign.

Palestine and Gaza

After the evacuation from Gallipoli Louis and the 1/5th spent about a month on Crete before arriving in Alexandria in Egypt on 1 February, initially to protect the Suez Canal from attack by the Turks. The Suez Canal provided a vital line of supply for Britain as it brought troops from India, Australia and New Zealand to the Western Front. The 1/5th, along with the rest of their Division, were moved here to discourage Turkish attempts to cut that supply line. They faced regular Turkish raids across the desert and in August 1916 they were called to more concerted action, successfully, in the Battle of Romani.

Louis and his comrades also had the opportunity to see the Pyramids, something that few Wigtown folk would have done. They also had the rather more dubious honour of managing the camels which supplied the troops with drinking water, apparently with a skill that rivalled the local Egyptians! Digging trenches in the hot, dry sand proved to be an arduous, repetitive and frustrating task for the Battalion. However, there was also time for recreation such as sea bathing and, of course, football. The latter required the construction of a full size pitch by removing the scrub and levelling the sand.

Whether Louis's footballing skills developed with Wigtown Utd were sufficient to merit inclusion in the team is not known but the standard would have been high with many men with League experience in the Battalion.

Allied commanders then decided that the best way to defend the Canal would be to advance further East and North to create a deeper buffer zone. That meant trying to capture Gaza. The initial attempt was unsuccessful so the Allies reinforced their forces and tried again. It was here, at the Second Battle of Gaza, that another of Louis McGuffie's Wigtown companions was killed. On 19 April 1917 the 1/5th were involved in a fierce, but unsuccessful, attack to take a Turkish position. At the end of the day 19 officers and 325 men from the Battalion were killed including Robert Knowles, aged 23, a tailor from Bladnoch. His death was followed three months later by that of William Kilpatrick, a father of two, also killed in action at Gaza.

The 1/5th were heavily involved in more action later in the year including a ferocious battle at Mughar in mid-November. It may have been here that Wigtown's Edward Clarke of the 1/5th was seriously wounded. He was evacuated to hospital at Kantara in Egypt where he died.

Further action followed in Palestine through 1917 and into 1918 before the 1/5th were transferred to the Western Front to help counter the German Spring offensive, arriving at Marseilles on 17 April 1918. Many officers and men had had no leave since they started for Gallipoli in 1915, three years earlier, and the arrival in France meant that, at long last, furlough was granted. However, 1918 was also the year that the Spanish Flu' epidemic took many lives across the world. The Battalion was badly hit: in June it had 9 officers (out of 39) and 206 other ranks (out of 826) laid low.

The Battalion fought their way through France and into Belgium. As the war entered its final weeks the 1/5th were fighting near the strategically important town of Wytschaete, not far from Ypres. It was here that Louis, having risen to the rank of Acting Sergeant, engaged in the action that would win him the Victoria Cross. The Battalion War Diary records that action:

The trench system where Louis fought was at Bayernwald. The photograph below shows how the system has recently been reconstructed as part of a local museum exhibit.

(Source: clevelode-battletours.com)

"*28 September: At 5.25 am our barrage came down along the front of the old French trench and along the Light Railway for 200 [yards] to the West of the broad gauge railway. The barrage, after 5 minutes, advanced at a rate of 100 [yards] each three minutes. At 5.25 am 2/ Lt Cairns advanced up to the barrage and followed it up to Piccadilly Farm supported by Lt Hyslop, taking prisoners 1 officer and 38 OR [Other Ranks] and 2 MGs [Machine Guns] before the 14th A&SH entered the farm. Casulaties that day 1 officer killed, OR 2 killed, 2 missing, 40 wounded.*"

The *London Gazette*, of 13 December 1918 provides the citation for the award of the Victoria Cross to Louis McGuffie:

"For most conspicuous bravery and resourceful leadership under heavy fire near Wytschaete on 28th September, 1918. During the advance to Piccadilly Farm, he, single-handed, entered several enemy dugouts and took many prisoners, and during subsequent operations dealt similarly with dugout after dugout, forcing one officer and twenty-five other ranks to surrender. During the consolidation of the first objective he pursued and brought back several of the enemy who were slipping away, and he was also instrumental in rescuing some British soldiers who were being led off as prisoners. Later in the day, when in command of a platoon, he led it with the utmost dash and resource, capturing many prisoners. This very gallant soldier was subsequently killed by a shell."

The photograph below shows one of the dugouts at Bayernwald.
As an interesting aside Adolf Hitler had been a runner in this trench system earlier in 1918, had been part of the German attacks on British positions and had won the Iron Cross.
(Source: www.webmatters.net)

G F Scott Elliot, in his book, "War History of the 5th Battalion King's Own Scottish Borderers", provides us with a little more detail of just what happened. In fact, Louis McGuffie showed exceptional courage and initiative on three separate occasions that day:

Around 5.30 am. "During the storming of [Piccadilly Farm] Sergeant McGuffie distinguished himself. His platoon commander was killed; he then took command, stormed several dugouts, and captured fully a dozen German prisoners, including two officers." *(pp 263)*. Around 7.30 am. "After Cairns had arrived at the St Eloi Road, Sergeant McGuffie saw a party of British prisoners being led off by a Bosche guard. Disregarding the possible consequences he dashed out, disarmed the Bosche escort single-handed, and released all the prisoners, who belong to another battalion." *(pp 264)*

And ...

> "Later in the day, when the Germans were holding up our advance by machine gun fire from a pillbox, he again ran forward and fired several rifle grenades through a loophole. Thus the pillbox and its garrison were captured." *pp 264*

Only a week after his brave exploits, on 4 October, while at Wytschaete, Louis McGuffie was killed.

Scott Elliot provides us with a little more background to the circumstances of Louis's death:

> "At 6 am on the 1st October the Battalion again moved forward by St Eloi and Lock Number 5 on the Ypres-Comines Canal to just north of San Voorde. The sun was shining during the day, and they bivouacked on the reverse slope of a hill which was comparatively dry.
>
> On the morning of the 2nd there was another advance to a wood just south of Kruiseik. The Battalion was in reserve to the 8th SR [Scottish Rifles] and 5th A&SH [Argyll and Sutherland Highlanders].
>
> Here we remained until the 6th. The bivouac area was severely shelled, and there were several casualties. It was here that Sergeant Louis McGuffie was killed, and this intrepid fighter never knew that he had won the most coveted honour that a soldier can possess." *pp 267*

Again, the Battalion War Diary gives some background to Louis's final days.

> "*30 September, Wytschaete. Rain fell all day and again the men had a bad time. Efforts were made and 4 hot meals and a rum ration were provided. A good deal of corrugated iron was found and 16 waterproof sheets and the men were more comfortable.*"
>
> "*3 October: Zandvoorde. A quiet day with a bright autumn sun. The men brightened up considerably. Communications in the wood improved. "A" Coy proceeded after dark to a wood [map co-ordinates A7 a 7.7] in reserve to the 5th A&SH. Field kitchens shelled with 4.2 in and 77 mm HE [High Explosives]. 1 casualty.*
>
> *4 October. The wood was shelled with 4.2 in and 77 mm. 2 killed, 4 wounded.*"

Louis McGuffie was laid to rest at Zandvoorde British Cemetery, 8 miles from Ypres. The cemetery was made after the Armistice when remains were brought in from the battlefields of the area.

1,583 servicemen of the First World War are buried or commemorated there. 1,135 of them are unidentified.

Louis's gravestone carries his name, regimental crest and representation of the Victoria Cross.

It also carries, at its foot, a personal message from his family taken from Alfred, Lord Tennyson's poem *Break, Break, Break*:

"OH FOR THE TOUCH
OF THE VANISHED HAND AND
THE SOUND OF THE VOICE
THAT IS STILL."

Louis McGuffie's Grave
(Source: www.warmemscot.s4.bizhat.com)

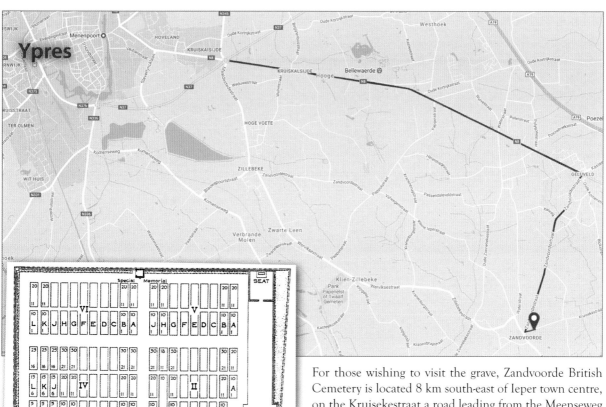

Zandvoorde Cemetery and location of Louis McGuffie's grave at Plot I.D12

For those wishing to visit the grave, Zandvoorde British Cemetery is located 8 km south-east of Ieper town centre, on the Kruisekestraat a road leading from the Meenseweg (N8), connecting Ypres (Ieper) to Menen. From Ypres town centre the Meenseweg is located via Torhoutstraat and right onto Basculestraat. Basculestraat ends at a main cross roads, directly over which begins the Meenseweg. 7.5 km along the Meenseweg in the village of Geluveld lies the right hand turning onto Zandvoordestraat. At the end of the Zandvoordestraat is the left hand turning onto Kruisekestraat. The cemetery itself is located 100 metres along the Kruisekestraat on the left hand side of the road. A map of the location can be found on the Commonwealth War Graves Commission's website at *www.cwgc.org/find-a-cemetery/cemetery/15904/zantvoorde-british-cemetery*

Military Records

Louis McGuffie had served with the King's Own Scottish Borderers for over four years. He had seen fierce action in Gallipoli, Palestine, France and Belgium. He died less than 40 days before the Armistice.

However, few military records for him remain. His enrolment papers and pension documents were destroyed, along with almost half of all World War One Army records, during the Blitz in the Second World War. Two documents do remain. First his medal index card: these records were created by the Army Medal Office towards the end of the First World War. They record the medals that men and women who served in the First World War were entitled to claim.

Most of the cards contain information about campaign medals, which were generally awarded to all those who served overseas. Louis's index card provides name, regiment, rank (Private then Acting Sergeant) and regimental number (original then later updated), the three campaign medals awarded (Victory Medal, British War Medal and 1915 Star).

The remarks indicate he was killed in action on 4 October 1918. Finally, the card records the first theatre of war Louis saw action in: 2B indicates the Balkans on 6 June 1915.

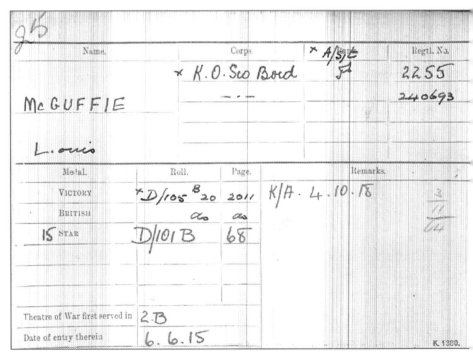

Louis McGuffie's Medal Index Card. (Source: Ancestry)

Register of Effects. *(Source: Ancestry)*

The other remaining document is taken from the Register of Soldiers' Effects. It provides name, regiment, rank, service number, date of death and recipient.

In Louis's case his mother, Catherine, received 4s 5d (22p), his final balance of pay. This seems a meagre amount: taking inflation into account it would be worth £13.77 today. Perhaps Louis had recently returned to the trenches following a period of leave.

So we have some documentary evidence of Louis's Army career and the citation for the award of the Victoria Cross. There can be no doubt about his bravery but little else in official records to show his character. We are fortunate, however, to have a first-hand account of him from someone who served alongside him, albeit briefly.

The book *"Tommy At War"* by John Saddler and Rosie Serdiville looks at soldiers' own stories of the Great War gleaned from letters home and personal diaries. It includes the story of an 18 year-old conscript, R A Urquhart, who was posted to the 5th Battalion KOSB. In August 1918 he and other new recruits joined their new battalion and were introduced to the acting Sergeant-Major, Louis McGuffie whose welcome included their first supply of tobacco and cigarettes. [There are no official records to corroborate Louis's temporary elevation to Sergeant-Major so this may be a mistake]. Urquhart records in his diary their advance over subsequent weeks against stiff German opposition and gives a first-hand account of Louis's leadership and bravery on 28 September, taking over command of the company when senior ranked officers were killed or wounded.

Urquhart gives his opinion of the VC award: "McGuffie deserved the VC", he says, "It is difficult to get to know officers and NCOs due to the high rate of change. At Wormhout he arranged my departure. I shall always remember his coolness and disregard for the German machine guns when he stood on the edge of the shell-hole."

("Tommy At War 1914-1918, The Soldier's Own Stories" pp 184).

4 - After the Armistice

The November 1918 Armistice silenced the guns of the "War to end all Wars". Louis McGuffie had died just days before the guns became silent.

Wigtown had lost around 50 local men; many more had returned home damaged physically or mentally, not least Louis's two brothers: Robert had lost an arm, while Edward John had been wounded in the ankle.

In the months following the Armistice, soldiers began to return and try to resume the quiet lives that they had given up to take part in the conflict. Others remained in the Army and casualties continued, largely due to illness.

Louis's story continued though.

Victoria Cross

On 21 December 1918 the Galloway Gazette announced the award of the Victoria Cross to Louis.

A month later it reported that Catherine McGuffie had been invited to Buckingham Palace to receive the Victoria Cross from the King and carried copies of the letters to her:

December 24 1918

Mrs C McGuffie
Wigtown

Dear Madam – Your son, the late sergeant Louis McGuffie, has, by the very gallant deeds he performed in September of this year, brought to his Battalion the highest honour that can be added to the records of any Regiment.

His Majesty The King has been pleased to approve of the posthumous award to your late son, of the Victoria Cross.

All of those who know of your son's extraordinary deeds of valour and of the great initiative and disregard for personal danger shown by him, recognise how thoroughly he deserved the great distinction now awarded him.

It is a great sorrow to all his colleagues that he could not have lived to receive their very sincere congratulations, and to march in their ranks wearing the decoration of which the whole Battalion is so justly proud.

All ranks desire to express to you their appreciation of the great honour your late son has brought to the Battalion, and their deep sympathy at your loss.

Yours sincerely
(sgd) F J Courtenay Hood
(Lieutenant-Colonel)
Commanding 1/5th Battalion KOSB

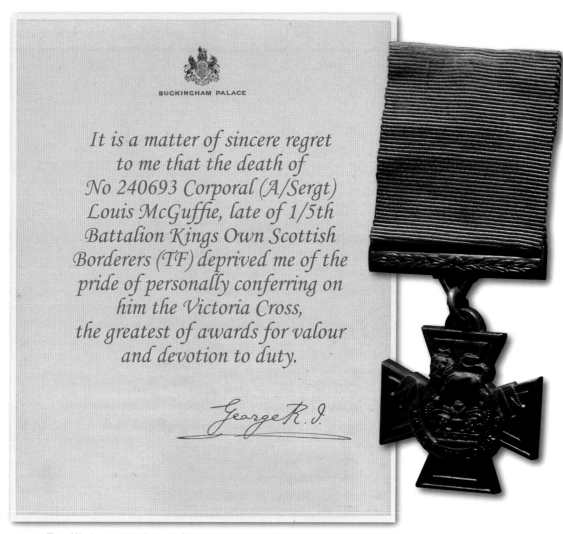

BUCKINGHAM PALACE

*It is a matter of sincere regret
to me that the death of
No 240693 Corporal (A/Sergt)
Louis McGuffie, late of 1/5th
Battalion Kings Own Scottish
Borderers (TF) deprived me of the
pride of personally conferring on
him the Victoria Cross,
the greatest of awards for valour
and devotion to duty.*

George R.I.

Text of His Majesty King George Vs letter sent to Louis's mother on 30 December 1918

Mrs McGuffie collects the VC

Catherine did not have the money to afford to travel to London to accept the Victoria Cross personally. In a gesture typical of the generosity of Wigtown's citizens a public collection paid for her travel to London. On her return to Wigtown she was met at the railway station by the whole town and she was paraded to the County Buildings with the Town Band playing in her honour.

The County Council also agreed to provide some money to help support her. The Galloway Gazette (10 May 1919) reported:

> "Provost Shaw said that it occurred to him that the County Council, being the most important body, might be willing to give general approval to a project which they had in hand in Wigtown, and the individual members might give their personal support to it. They were raising a small fund for the benefit of the widowed mother of the Wigtown VC winner. He was the only one in the county who had succeeded in winning that great distinction, and, unfortunately, he had been killed within a few days after his meritorious deeds. The meeting approved of the project."

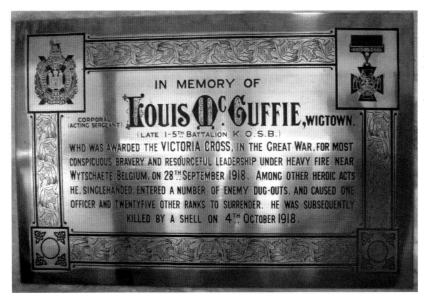

In a further gesture of the Burgh's pride a brass plaque, paid for by public subscription, was erected in the County Buildings in Louis's honour: it can still be seen there today.

McGuffie memorial in County Buildings

The plaque's unveiling was reported in *The Scotsman* (6 December 1920):

> Wigtown - An interesting and impressive ceremony was performed in the county town of Wigtown on Saturday, when the Right Hon. Sir H. E. Maxwell, Bart., Lord-Lieutenant of the county, unveiled a beautiful brass tablet on a granite background in the County Buildings, Wigtown, in memory of Corporal (Acting Sergeant) Louis McGaffie *(sic)*, Wigtown, late of the 1/5th Battalion K.O.S.B., who was awarded the Victoria Cross for most conspicuous bravery and resourceful leadership under heavy fire near Wytschaete, Belgium, on September 28, 1918. The memorial was erected by Sir Peter McClelland, a native of Wigtown. There was a large attendance at the unveiling, which included a contingent from the Newton-Stewart Comrades of the Great War, under command of Captain McNeill and Captains Brand and Salmond. At the close of the ceremony several of the men of the parish who had also won distinctions in the war were presented with watches in recognition of their services.

The white information board alongside it is a much more recent addition.

Wigtown War Memorial

Two months after the Armistice a public meeting was held in the town to discuss a suitable way of commemorating the sacrifice made by the servicemen of the Burgh. A range of options was considered including a cottage hospital to serve the Machars, a mechanics' institute or a monument.

A committee of the Town Council was set up to take the matter forward. As is the way with committees, progress appeared slow with options for the location and design of the memorial still undecided in early 1922.

*The Opening of
the War Memorial
(Photograph courtesy of
David McNally)*

below:
The War Memorial today

The opening ceremony was finally held on 8 October 1922 with a huge crowd of between 2,000 and 3,000 watching.

Over 230 men (and at least two women) with Wigtown connections had served their country in the Great War. The memorial contains the names of 54 men from the Burgh who were killed (although there are at least 30 more with Wigtown connections whose names are not included). There are a further 13 casualties from the Second World War. All are listed in alphabetical order with no distinction of rank, regiment or honours gained. *(see Appendix 4).*

Despite the Armistice Wigtown soldiers still died as a consequence of the conflict whether from illnesses or their wounds in the subsequent months and years.

Remembrance Day 2017

Thomas Cromie died from the Spanish Flu epidemic.

John Davies died in 1920 in a Staffordshire hospital for those suffering from shellshock.

David Boyd, from the 1/5th KOSB, died in 1927 aged 49. His gravestone in Wigtown High Cemetery states he was "disabled in the Great War".

Louis's own brother, Robert, had lost an arm (though it did not prevent him from shooting the wildfowl prolific to the area using a punt gun to compensate for the loss of a limb).

For others the damage was psychological rather than physical. In his book about crofting life at Torhousemuir, Joe Whiteford, describing the inhabitants of the community says,

"The Lindsays farmed Meadowbank … the surviving son, Peter, had been gassed or shell-shocked in World War 1, stuttered and had a habit of repeating his questions constantly."

Wigtown's women had lost husbands, fathers and brothers; children had lost their father; families were shattered. A poignant photograph of the time shows the Clark family - mother, father and three daughters who had each lost their sweethearts in the war.

Louis McGuffie's was not the only act of bravery from Wigtown soldiers that received official recognition (*see Appendix 5*). Recovery from the Great War in Wigtown, as in communities across Britain, indeed across the world, would be slow but the horrors experienced were insufficient to prevent further conflict.

5 - The Present Day

Louis McGuffie's medals on display at the KOSB Museum in Berwick.

Some years ago Robert McGuffie presented his brother's medals to the KOSB Museum in Berwick where they can still be seen on display. The photograph above shows, from left to right: the Victoria Cross and three campaign medals - the 1914-15 Star, the British War Medal and the Victory Medal. Below is the Memorial Plaque that was issued to Catherine McGuffie after the War. The plaques were made of bronze, and hence popularly known as the "Dead Man's Penny", because of the similarity in appearance to the somewhat smaller penny coin. They were sent to the next-of-kin of all British and Empire service personnel who were killed as a result of the war.

Commemorative Paving Stone and Memorial Gardens

In August 2013 the Government announced that commemorative paving stones would be laid in the home towns of every UK soldier awarded a Victoria Cross during World War 1. 628 VCs were awarded to 627 recipients during the war, 68 to Scots.

The commemorative stone for Louis McGuffie will be located at the entrance to the town gardens, opposite the County Buildings. In addition, townsfolk have felt it appropriate to name the town's gardens after Louis and commissioned an entrance gateway from local artist, Jack Sloan.

LOUIS McGUFFIE VC
1893-1918
"ONCE A BORDERER, ALWAYS A BORDERER"

Appendix 1: The McGuffies

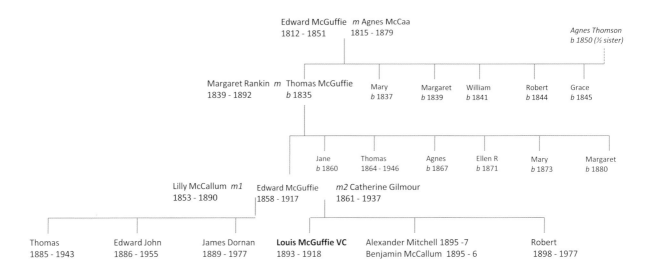

Appendix 2: The Gilmours

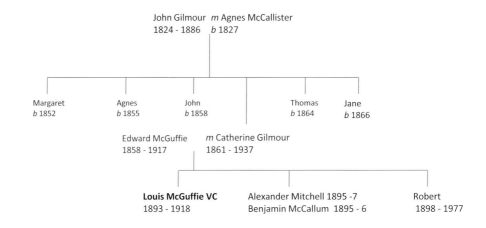

Appendix 3: The McCallums

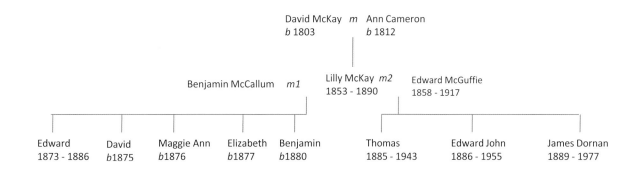

David McKay *m* Ann Cameron
b 1803   *b* 1812

Benjamin McCallum   *m1*   Lilly McKay *m2*   Edward McGuffie
                                    1853 - 1890   1858 - 1917

| Edward | David | Maggie Ann | Elizabeth | Benjamin | Thomas | Edward John | James Dornan |
| 1873 - 1886 | *b*1875 | *b*1876 | *b*1877 | *b*1880 | 1885 - 1943 | 1886 - 1955 | 1889 - 1977 |

Appendix 4 - Wigtown War Memorial - World War I Casualties

Name	Age	Regiment	Date of Death
John Black	24	Tank Corps	23/8/1918
William Black	30	Royal Scots Fusiliers	16/9/1916
Robert Boyd	37	Royal Scots Fusiliers	7/4/1917
Andrew Briggs	22	Cameron Highlanders	11/4/1917
John Briggs	20	Highland Light Infantry	31/10/1914
Alexander Broadfoot	28	Canadian Infantry	8/11/1917
Edward Clark	22	King's Own Scottish Borderers	17/11/1917
John Coburn	19	Gordon Highlanders	24/9/1917
Robert Copland	30	Highland Light Infantry	29/3/1918
Thomas Cromie	21	Tank Corps	17/2/1919
William Edwards	47	King's Own Scottish Borderers	12/7/1915
John Ewing	23	Cameron Highlanders	19/4/1918
John Flynn	23	Royal Scots Fusiliers	11/11/1914
Edward Hale	23	Army Cyclist Corps	5/10/1918
James Hargreaves	18	King's Own Scottish Borderers	18/8/1918
John Harvey	24	Highland Light Infantry	3/7/1916
Adam Horner	37	Royal Garrison Artillery	1/8/1917
Robert Hughes	19	The Black Watch	2/7/1917
William Irvine	39	Royal Field Artillery	3/9/1917
William Jamieson	24	Cameronians (Scottish Rifles)	9/6/1917
David Kellie	24	Cameron Highlanders	3/4/1917
Francis Kennedy	31	King's Own Scottish Borderers	10/4/1918
Leslie Kennedy	24	Highland Light Infantry	9/7/1916
Edward Kilpatrick	20	King's Own Scottish Borderers	4/7/1915
William Kilpatrick	26	King's Own Scottish Borderers	14/8/1917
David Kiltie		Royal Naval Division	N/K
Alexander Knowles	32	King's Own Scottish Borderers	1/9/1918
Robert Knowles	23	King's Own Scottish Borderers	19/4/1917
Charles Landers	22	Royal Scots Fusiliers	8/7/1919
Alexander Laurie	25	Canadian Infantry	6/6/1916
James Loan	24	Scots Guards	16/5/1915
James Love	26	Royal Scots Fusiliers	30/7/1916

Blain Malone	40	Loyal Lancashire Regiment	11/7/1917
David Malone	21	Royal Naval Volunteer Reserve	11/10/1918
Robert Murray	33	The Black Watch	21/1/1916
David McCaskie	25	Highland Light Infantry	29/4/1917
Thomas McCaskie	25	King's Own Scottish Borderers	7/11/1915
Thomas McCheyne	26	Canadian Infantry	26/4/1916
Ernest McClelland	25	Cameron Highlanders	24/11/1916
James McCulloch	34	Gordon Highlanders	13/11/1916
Louis McGuffie	25	King's Own Scottish Borderers	4/10/1918
Charles McKinna	25	Argyll & Sutherland Highlanders	1/8/1917
James McNeil	22	King's Own Scottish Borderers	14/7/1915
Joseph McRobert	21	Argyll & Sutherland Highlanders	28/10/1918
Hugh Neil	32	Royal Army Service Corps	27/12/1917
William Paton	43	Royal Army Service Corps	19/2/1919
Stanley Rolfe	25	Queen's Westminster Rifles	10/9/1916
Walter Scott	24	Highland Light Infantry	28/10/1918
William Sproul	34	Machine Gun Corps	20/6/1918
George Todd	20	Cameronians (Scottish Rifles)	6/3/1917
William Walker	24	Royal Air Force	8/10/1918
Charles Boyd	19	Cameron Highlanders	14/11/1914
John Davies	26	Royal Army Service Corps	13/4/1920
David McMurray	32	Australian Infantry	9/10/1917

Appendix 5: Wigtown's Other Winners of Gallantry Medals

Military Cross

William Ian McKeand. Captain, Lancashire Infantry Brigade. For gallant service in France.
(William McKeand survived the war.)

Distinguished Flying Cross and Croix de Guerre (Belgium)

William Walker. Captain, 6 Squadron, Royal Air Force. Awarded the Belgian Croix de Guerre in April 1918.

The award of the Distinguished Flying Cross was reported in the London Gazette of 2/11/1918:

"Lieut. (T./Capt.) William Walker. On August 9th accurate information as to the whereabouts of our cavalry patrols was urgently required; Captain Walker undertook to obtain this. After patrolling for three hours at a very low altitude, subjected to intense machine-gun fire, he brought back the requisite information. This officer had already completed two previous reconnaissances that day, and on the day before he had flown for six and a half hours engaging enemy aeroplanes and troops. A striking example of courage, endurance and devotion to duty"
(William Walker was killed in action on 8/10/1918. His body was not found and he is named on the Arras Flying Services Memorial.)

Distinguished Conduct Medal

Martin McGeoch. Lance-Corporal, Scottish Horse. Award of medal reported in Galloway Gazette: "He won the medal for gallant conduct at Gallipoli while acting as an orderly to the medical officer of the regiment. On five different occasions he went out under heavy shell fire, dressed wounds, and brought in wounded men of other units".
(Martin McGeoch survived the war and resumed his career as a school teacher.)

Military Medal

Alexander Broadfoot. Private 130245, Canadian Infantry. Twice mentioned in despatches and awarded MM for daring work as a runner in the assault on Vimy Ridge. (*Alexander Broadfoot died of wounds 8 November 1917 and is buried at Etaples.*)

Thomas Caldwell Cromie. Private 95248, Tank Corps. Citation from Tank Corps records. "On October 8 1918 at Serain he drove a whippet tank entirely new to him with the greatest gallantry and coolness for seven hours. At one time his tank developed mechanical trouble which he successfully mended under shell fire. Later, his skill undoubtedly saved his machine while it was under heavy shell fire, and his courage and devotion to duty were an example to the rest of the crew. He succeeded in bringing his tank to its objective in spite of great difficulties, such as railways and sunken roads, and enabled the gunners to do considerable execution amongst the enemy." (*Thomas Cromie died of broncho-pneumonia in Spring 1919 aged 21 and is buried at St Pol.*)

Robert Douglas. Company Sergeant Major, Gordon Highlanders. Awarded Military Medal during retreat from Mons. (*Robert Douglas survived the war and worked at Bladnoch Distillery and Creamery. Took charge of Wigtown company of Home Guard in WW2.*)

James William Eric Goldie Ker. Private 1529, 1/5th King's Own Scottish Borderers. No details of circumstances of award. Also awarded Croix de Guerre. (*James Ker survived the war and emigrated to Australia*).

Harry Duncan. Lance-Corporal 22644, Argyll & Sutherland Highlanders. Copy of report from Commanding Officer: "Near Joncourt (near St Quentin) on 30th September 1918, this NCO with a small party became cut off, but held on to his post until another battalion counter-attacked through him. He and his party had in the meantime inflicted heavy casualties on the enemy, and by so doing had prevented him from working round our flank. This NCO on several subsequent occasions distinguished himself on patrol, bringing back most useful information. He showed great courage and initiative throughout the entire operations." (*Harry Duncan survived the War*).

John McHarrie. Lance Corporal 292364, 8th Gordon Highlanders. No details of circumstances of award. Wounded and prisoner of war for 10 months. (*After the war John McHarrie served in the Royal Irish Constabulary for two years before returning to Wigtownshire. He died in 1938 aged 48*).

Meritorious Service Medal

Arthur Todd. Corporal, Australian Imperial Force. Extract from Corps' orders of 3 August 1916: "The Commanding Officer has much pleasure in recording and bringing to notice the gallant and meritorious conduct of No 1536 A/Cpl A. R. Todd, Australian Cyclists. This NCO, while participating in the practice of live grenade throwing this afternoon, picked up and threw out of reach a live grenade which had been dropped among five men, and was in immediate danger of exploding. By his act of coolness and courage Corpl Todd undoubtedly saved many men's lives." (*Arthur Todd survived the war and returned to Australia where he married and raised a family.*)

Bibliography

"Albanich: A History of the Galloway Rifle Volunteers"
by Ian Devlin. Published by GC Book Publishers Ltd.
ISBN 1 872350 07 0

"Old Wigtown"
by Jack Hunter.
Published by Stenlake Publishing.
ISBN 1 84033 025 2

"Answering the Call: Auchencairn and The First World War"
by Stuart Wilson.
Published by Dander Publishing.
ISBN 978-0-9562168-0-9

"Through the Lens: Glimpses of Old Wigtownshire".
Published by Dumfries and Galloway Council.
ISBN 0 946280 53 3

"Torhousemuir: Memories of a Wigtownshire Crofter 1935-1945"
by Joe Whiteford.
Published by Dumfries & Galloway Council.
ISBN 0 946280 54 1

"War History of the 5th Battalion King's Own Scottish Borderers"
by G F Scott Elliot.
Published 1928 by Robert Dinwiddie, Dumfries.

"Tommy at War: 1914-1918, The Soldiers' Own Stories"
by John Sadler and Rosie Serdiville.
Published by The Robson Press.
ISBN 978-1-84954-514-3

"Wigtown's Historic Buildings"
Published by GC Book Publishers.
ISBN 1 872350 83 6